(I.S.S.E.)

Inspiration story solution excellent results

HOW I LOST **100**LBS WEIGHT

Disclaimer

Table of Contents

Disclaimer iii

INTRODUCTION 7

CHAPTER ONE: INSPIRATION FOR WEIGHT LOSS 9

INSPIRATION 9

BACKGROUND 14

What are Gallstones? 16

Common Symptoms of Gallstones 16

Key risks factors for Gallstone formation 17

Health and Physical Challenges 17

How Can I Lose Weight? 19

Why am I doing this? 19

My Simply Stay Away (SSA) List 22

CHAPTER TWO: MY STORY 23

BACKGROUND 24

CHAPTER THREE: Solution 32

CHAPTER FOUR: Excellent result 46

INTRODUCTION

Former American president, Ronald Reagan, enjoyed recounting the story about how he learnt the hard way to make firm decisions. He shared his story that once his aunt sent him to a cobbler to have a pair of shoes made for him when he was young. When the shoemaker asked, 'Do you want a square toe or a round toe one?' he hemmed and hawed, so the cobbler said, 'Come back in a day or two and tell me what you want.' Later the cobbler saw Reagan on the street and asked him about his decision for the shoes. 'I haven't made up my mind yet,' he responded. 'Very well,' the cobbler said, 'your shoes will be ready tomorrow.' When Reagan got the shoes, one had a round toe, and the other had a square toe! Reagan said, 'Looking at those shoes every day taught me a lesson. If you don't make your own decisions, somebody, something or a condition will make them for you.'

The truth is, at some point in our lives, we would face situations that will require us to make vital decisions that can affect our life in both ways, positively or negatively. Interestingly, people tend not to decide, which mostly ends up in a way that they do not like or have much control over, especially when it relates to managing your weight/obesity. The outcome usually has a rippling effect that primarily affects your health which, in turn, will affect other areas such as your family, relationships, business, etc.

In my case, I developed some unhealthy habits with the time that led me towards gaining weight over the years. I took a small step to make some efforts for losing weight. I

(I.S.S.E.)

Inspiration story solution excellent results

tried going to the gym, taking dietary supplements and other quick-fix measures, but it did not work out for me. At first, I became desperate, but when it didn't turn out as expected, I was discouraged. I fell back to my old habits and ended up putting more weight. My BMI labelled me as OBESE by then.

When I reflected upon my poor health that resulted from excessive weight, I made a commitment to myself to work for it. With a reading of 7.9, my reports were pointing towards a high level of cholesterol. GALLSTONES made it worst. I suffered from severe abdominal cramps that led me to the hospital admissions and eventually, Surgery. After the surgery, I knew that I had to make a conscious decision to begin my weight loss journey. My determination totally changed my life and resulted in positive outcomes.

The book is about my journey. I have compiled my Inspiration, Story, Solution and the excellent results that I achieved, in the form of a book that interestingly condenses to my name: ISSE.

I believe that as you will read my story, inspiration, guiding wisdom, challenges/struggles and detailed information with advice on how I lost a total of 45kg within a 12-month period in this book, you will make up your mind to begin your journey. In addition, I have also shared some vital tips that helped me in my journey, and I believe it will be useful to you as well. This book will give you the courage and determination not only to begin your own weight loss journey but also making it simpler as it did for me.

CHAPTER ONE: INSPIRATION FOR WEIGHT LOSS

INSPIRATION

Inspiration is said to be a process of being mentally stimulated to do something. Putting it together in terms of emotions, it often depicts enthusiasm and taking action in pursuit of a particular endeavor. In this case, Inspiration is the enthusiasm and losing weight is that particular endeavor. The keywords here, as it relates to weight loss, are:

1. Being mentally stimulated to do something and;
2. Taking action in pursuit of a particular endeavour

Being honest about enthusiasm, I cannot promise that there will be a lot of it at the beginning of your weight loss journey, but one thing I can promise is that as you begin to notice little results, your enthusiasm will boost automatically. It will push you to keep up with your commitment to continuing your journey.

You need to understand one thing that it is a Journey; this term implies that it involves a process and will take a while. Therefore, to keep myself mentally stimulated and stay

(I.S.S.E.)

Inspiration story solution excellent results committed throughout the process, I had to come to terms with a few useful thoughts of wisdom that kept my inspiration alive throughout my journey.

They are as follows:

1. You must have a clear vision

A clear vision holds a valuable place in most things we do in our lives because achieving clarity of vision through self-awareness opens the door to endless possibilities. The same formula works for weight loss. You need to have a clear vision or picture of what you want to look like right from the start of your journey. The reason behind this is that a clear vision will help you to focus on your decisions, which in turn gives you the grounds to base your decision on.

For example, if you have a choice between a healthy bowl of porridge or a sausage roll for breakfast, then the vision or picture of your Fit version would help you make the right decision.

2. You must become completely self-aware

Success in the weight loss journey depends a lot on your self-awareness and the excess weight you have to deal with. You must be willing to carry out an honest and realistic assessment of yourself and the factors that caused the excessive weight, without a bias.

Like following directions from Google map or using the satellite navigator in any automobile, you need to know your starting drop off prior to the start of the journey. In this way, you would be able to, consciously identify your

(I.S.S.E.)
Inspiration story solution excellent results strengths, weakness, habits, formed patterns, obstacles and power that could help you prevent excess weight gain. Instantly, you will be able to lay the foundation for solving the challenges because you would be able to identify the do's and donts' to focus on.

You would need to check out what led you to the excessive weight in terms of:

- ✓ Knowledge - that you possess or was lacking before
- ✓ Skills - that I had or lacked which could have made a difference
- ✓ Attitude/actions - that I take or avoided which led me to the current state

It is important to note that the core of self-awareness lies in taking responsibility for the quality of your life. Achieving clarity of vision through self-awareness can open the door to endless possibilities.

3. Set your goal and stay focused

In order to achieve your weight loss vision, you need to have a goal. Setting goals is extremely important and crucial in succeeding this journey. Remember, the goal should be realistic. Keep your focus intact by pushing yourself towards taking actions daily for achieving that goal. The real value of reaching a goal does not lie in the result achieved but, in the journey, that you've finished and the person you have become now.

The journey will not be easy; therefore, you must have both:

(I.S.S.E.)

Inspiration story solution excellent results

- Long-term goals - the big picture or target results you want to achieve over a long period of time, let's say 6 months – 1year.
- Short-term goals - Smaller actions that you have to take daily, weekly and monthly if you are serious about your long-term goals.

So, whenever you feel that you cannot carry on further, remember the reasons behind pursuing this journey and what you wished to accomplish at the end because pain is just temporary, it does not last forever but the results would. For sure. Most times, the bad habits that resulted in your weight gain cannot be changed overnight; you need to take calculated steps and action to implement the needed change.

4. Stay motivated

You can define self-motivation as "the force that drives you to do things". It is the feeling that pushes you to work towards your goals. While dealing with obstacles in the weight loss journey, it will be your self-motivation that help you to carry on.

Wanting to lose weight is not enough. After setting your goal, you need to crave for it and take charge of it in an unstoppable manner. Obstacles will invariably show up along the journey, but your self-motivation must be absolutely compelling. You will need to:

- ✓ Remind yourself the reason for starting this journey – which for me was my deteriorating health and the happiness of my family
- ✓ Review your goals at least twice daily
- ✓ Develop and focus on good and supportive habits

(I.S.S.E.)
Inspiration story solution excellent results
- ✓ Practice positive thinking because positive thoughts go a long way in helping you to regain your balance when you fall

Being positively motivated is the best possible way to get through your weight problems. Never forget that losing weight is a journey that consists of low and high days.

5. Practice the celebration of Successful Milestones

Success is simply achieving the goal you set out to do: big or small. As simple as the celebration of successful milestones is, it can go a long way to impact on your mindset and the overall success of your weight loss journey.

The message behind this lovely saying, "Success comes from simplicity," is not over-emphasized, for most of the time, it can create the greatest impact. So, as you practice the simple act of celebrating small successful milestones, you will find out that you are encouraged and motivated to continue the journey, which ultimately creates an impact on the overall outcome of your weight loss journey.

It is important to know that the success you are celebrating is not about how many people appreciate your work, it is about how honest you were to yourself and the heart and soul you put into achieving your result. Therefore, in the next chapter, I will be talking about my story discussing what inspired me to start my weight loss journey and how I lost 100 lb. weight within a year.

(I.S.S.E.)

Inspiration story solution excellent results

BACKGROUND

I grew up in an ethnic culture where good and pleasurable food, which is not necessarily healthy, played a significant role in our lives. I began to enjoy my food so much that putting on weight did not seem like an issue for me. In fact, food was a part of most things. All types of foods, regardless of their nutritional value, were consumed at any time of the day. Sugary, oily, fleshy and unhealthy foods are served on every occasion.

This doesn't end here. When you visit friends and relatives, they consider it very disrespectful if you decline food offered to you irrespective of your diet plan. We just enjoyed food with or without a good company. "Food is life" was the actual message we were following, I guess.

Over the years, I gained so much weight, for which I never bothered as long as my food was pleasurable to me. However, with time, I became dissatisfied with my weight. I wanted to get rid of it. Despite all my efforts, nothing worked for me. I thought I was following the correct plan to lose weight, such as going to the gym regularly and taking different dietary supplements. Later on, I realized that most of my efforts were not adequate for me. It turned out to be a complete waste of time and money and obviously affected my motivation. In a while, I gave up and was back to where I started.

I tried dieting for a short time of period, which seemed too hard to keep up with, and I fell back to old unhealthy habits. I was so desperate to lose weight. I wasn't able to figure out what was I doing wrong? I thought I was moving in the correct direction. I was finding it difficult to understand my body system. I gained twice as much as I lost every time. I was quite frustrating.

I realized this was going to be one of the most challenging life tasks I had to face. I thought to myself, "why is weight so easy to gain, yet it's hard to lose"? It is definitely, because of the popular saying, "an old habit dies hard". I gained so much weight that according to the BMI, I was officially falling in the category of obese. I should have done something about it, but I did not take any concrete action until something drastic happened.

In 2014, it was summers, I started to begin a sudden intense pain in my abdomen that usually lasted over an hour. The pain was excruciating to the extent that I had to go for medical examination where my fear became apparent. I was diagnosed with a high level of cholesterol reading of 7.9. The cause behind the pain was Gallstones formed due to cholesterol. This condition triggered an intense abdominal pain that usually lasts around 1 to 5 hours. This pain is known as Biliary Colic and is mostly treated with painkillers that I used often to ease the pain, but that wasn't the cure. I decided to find out more about GALLSTONES.

What are Gallstones?

They are not actual stones; they are pieces of solid particles formed of bile, cholesterol, and bilirubin in the gallbladder (a small pear-shaped sack-like organ located under the liver in the upper right part of the abdomen). These stones are

(I.S.S.E.)

Inspiration story solution excellent results formed when the amount of cholesterol in the bile is elevated. You might not even have a clue for their presence until they block a bile duct, thereby causing much pain, which would require immediate medical treatment.

Gallstone varies in sizes and actually becomes a problem when one or more of the stone clogs the opening of the duct outside the gallbladder. This can trigger a sudden intense abdominal pain that usually known as Biliary Colic.

Common Symptoms of Gallstones

Following are few symptoms pointing towards gallstones that are not relieved by over the counter medications:

- ✓ Intense abdominal pain
- ✓ Fever and sweating
- ✓ Chills
- ✓ Jaundice
- ✓ Nausea and vomiting

Key risks factors for Gallstone formation

It is also important to point out the main two key factors that could lead to the formation of cholesterol gallstones. Usually, our focus is mainly on the first factor while the second should also be taken into consideration, especially when you commence your weight loss journey:

- ✓ Being overweight
- ✓ Rapid weight loss on a crash or starvation diet

Health and Physical Challenges

Over time, I started experiencing such intense pain resulting from gallbladder attacks that I could not breathe properly. The pain is commonly located at your back, either between your shoulder blades or in your right shoulder. I was experiencing all the earlier mentioned symptoms. The pain bugged me in the middle of the night. The only remedy was painkillers that provided little or no help since the pain was so intense and unbearable.

The Pain got so worse that I end up in hospital and surgery was the only viable option available to save my life. After surgery, I asked the doctor what caused the problem; the doctor told me all was the diet-related problem, resulting from long-term bad eating habits.

Due to all these health problems, I spent a lot of time going in and out of the hospital. I can recall coming out of the operating room one new year's eve, the moment I opened my eyes, all I heard was doctors and nurse saying to each other the new year's greetings, while lying on the hospital bed, it suddenly dawned on me that the blame for my condition was all on me. I decided to do something about my problem as soon as I recover. At all cost, I must do something proactive to reduce and monitor my weight, which will over time, improve my health.

I have had enough of being overweight, I decide, if I don't change my lifestyle and eating habits, I will probably end in the hospital again with an even worsened situation, I have suffered enough in the past due to my negligence in handling my health challenges.

A second encounter I had, which I call the 'Icing on the cake' that made me realize that the negligence of my health does not only affect me but also my family/loved ones. It happened on a fateful day when my little princess came up to me and said "dad I love you so much, you went through a lot in the past due to your health, it had a serious effect on us, so I do not want to lose you. Is it ok if you can shed or lose some weight?" I was shocked. She concluded by saying in a joking manner; "dad, you look like my granddad, please make sure you look like my dad soon, everyone thinks you are my granddad". This conversation was life-changing for me; it inspired me, even more, to do something urgently about my weight and health.

At that moment, I felt disappointed in myself. I have let the family and myself down. My kids were concerned about my health. I looked at her and said, "Don't worry princess, this time I will make sure that I look like your dad, not your granddad". She replied; "that would be a dream come true for me".

The game was on, and I was ever so determined. From that day onward, I had no choice but to engage myself in the pursuit of my weight loss agenda. I did some research on how to lose weight in a healthy way, no more supplement or shortcuts. I realized the process of losing weight takes time and requires patience to succeed, and there's no need to rush.

How Can I Lose Weight?

Questions began to spring up in my mind, what do I do next? Where do I go? Whom do I believe? If I do not take the necessary action, now history will repeat itself. I was in a desperate situation and ready to do whatever it takes.

I failed miserably in the past, I cannot afford to fail this time around, the word failure had to be sponged from my dictionary, no more excuses, no lazier approach towards my intended project, I knew it was going be very challenging, so I had to put my head down and face my

(I.S.S.E.)

Inspiration story solution excellent results

fears

Fear as an abbreviation has two meanings (false, evidence appealing real) or (fear, everything, and run), so I decided to face my biggest fear and accept all the challenges that come along with it. I knew it would not be easy, but I was willing to sacrifice my comfort to achieve my goals. I had to improve myself a little every single day, and eventually, there will be some significant changes for sure.

Why am I doing this?

I am doing this for my family and most importantly for myself, so I can live a healthy, long and happy life with my family. From July 15th 2017, I started my weight loss journey, this fruitful journey that has changed my life for good, and I will never forget that day. This time there is no such thing as giving up or going back, no excuses, junk food and no more laziness. Action as is popularly said "speaks louder than words". On that faithful day, I embarked on my mission with a positive mindset. After a year of perseverance, hard work while striving to make the mark, I began to notice that, I have become very energetic and light. It came to my realization that I was shedding fat and shedding weight like never before; the results were amazing and very fulfilling. Close friends and family members started noticing the wonderful change, after a year of determination, hard work and rigorous routine from 15 July 2017 to 15 July 2018, I shed 100 lb. (45Kg) of my weight.

After a year of committed hard work, I was finally happy because I could see the difference and attest to the visible results of my labour, I had to empty out my wardrobe

(I.S.S.E.)

Inspiration story solution excellent results
simply because my clothes no longer fit me. On a particular occasion, I attended the parents and teacher association at my kid's school, and the teachers could hardly recognize me. They actually thought I was someone else, all of sudden I was at the centre of attention, and everyone wanted to know how I manage to lose so much in such a short space of time. My own neighbours also could not recognize me.

At another occasion, while I was on a trip, I was stopped by immigration passport control, I have pulled aside for questioning to confirm my identity. It took them a while to confirm, but at the end of the exercise, they realized that I was the same person on the passport who has undergone a little transformation. I had to explain that I lost so much weight as a health precaution. The officer recommended that I update my passport photo. This time around, I did not disappoint my family or myself. I felt like the wealthiest man in the world, as they say; your health is your wealth.

Based on my success so far, I would be sharing my understanding and knowledge garnered in my quest to lose weight and how I succeeded in such a short time. One of the reasons I decided to write this book is for other people to understand how I did it and what informed my decision to take action and if possible apply the same formula as I did to get that astounding results.

What helped me most was a determination for taking the necessary and prompt actions. Secondly, focusing on how to achieve my vision every day also helped. I had to plan and actively pursue my daily, weekly, monthly and annual goals. Even when I was knocked down in life, the only choice that I had was to get up and move forward, and I realised I do not have time to waste. I decided to wake up every day at the same time, exactly 5:30, start with meditation for 10 minutes; this is how I used to meditate:

- ✓ Take a 5-seconds long deep breath, and then hold it for 5 seconds, then breathe out slowly for 5 seconds,
- ✓ Do the actions for a set of 11 rounds, then clear your head while meditating. It helped me improve my focus.

Thirdly, I had to focus on the present and not the past, I knew exactly what my number one goal was, so I always kept that in mind and fit it into my daily lifestyle schedules. It became a habit, 10 minutes' meditation, after which I will go for an hour walk. I started from the basic, and gradually I worked my way up, first thing first, I do drink a glass of mineral water before I start walking, when I am done, I will then have my breakfast, which is a finger of banana, two boiled eggs and glass of water. For lunch, it would be a hand full of couscous vegetables such as chickpeas, broccoli, carrots, sweet corn, spinach, chicken breast with skin off, fish and plain water, and for dinner, I would have one apple or orange and plain water. I did this consistently for a year!

For a year? You might ask, yes for a year. Sometimes in life, you need to push yourself beyond the boundaries and out of your comfort zone in order to achieve your goals, and this would not be easy. I used to go to the gym 3 times during the week with my coach William Canty who helped me a lot. Coaches help you reach your goals faster. In life,

(I.S.S.E.)

Inspiration story solution excellent results whether you are doing business or losing weight, having a coach to motivate and direct makes a lot of difference. I believe that with their help, you can reach your goals faster. I tried to lose weight in the past and failed so many times, failure is not a bad thing though, you just learn and grow from it, I never gave up although I failed many times in the past. I learned a lot from my failures, and finally, I lost 100 lbs. within a year! For me, that was the biggest achievement! All the struggles I went through, and the hard work paid off, pain is just temporary; it does not last forever. Now I am happy with my life.

My Simply Stay Away (SSA) List

At the onset of and through your weight loss journey, you would need to stay away from the following:

- ❖ Deep Frying: such as chips. Chicken burger, lamb burger, beef burger, lamb donner, chicken donner, crisps etc.
- ❖ Sweets: cupcake, biscuit, ice cream, chocolate bars, Muffin, cake etc.
- ❖ Drinks: energy drinks, Lucozade, Red bull, Coca-Cola, 7up. Fanta, Mirinda, Pepsi coke, diet coke, juice, alcohol etc.
- ❖ Flour: white bread, pasta, pizza, breadstick, cereals, cookies, crackers etc.

I do understand how difficult it is to stay away from these types of foods. Apply these rules and follow it rigorously, and you will see that big change that you have dedicated your resources to attain. So you have two options, you can either take unflinching action or forget about losing weight. If you really want to have real changes in your life, do not wait for it. I know one thing for sure, you can get your physique into what you desire, but self-discipline and

(I.S.S.E.)
Inspiration story solution excellent results
consistency are indispensable tools. More solutions will be
discussed in the next chapter.

CHAPTER TWO: MY STORY

BACKGROUND

I grew up in an ethnic culture where good and pleasurable food, which is not necessarily healthy, played a significant role in our lives. I began to enjoy my food so much that putting on weight did not seem like an issue for me. In fact, food was a part of most things. All types of foods, regardless of their nutritional value, were consumed at any time of the day. Sugary, oily, fleshy and unhealthy foods are served on every occasion.

This doesn't end here. When you visit friends and relatives, they consider it very disrespectful if you decline food offered to you irrespective of your diet plan. We just enjoyed food with or without a good company. "Food is life" was the actual message we were following, I guess.

Over the years, I gained so much weight, for which I never bothered as long as my food was pleasurable to me. However, with time, I became dissatisfied with my weight. I wanted to get rid of it. Despite all my efforts, nothing worked for me. I thought I was following the correct plan to lose weight, such as going to the gym regularly and taking different dietary supplements. Later on, I realized that most of my efforts were not adequate for me. It turned out to be a complete waste of time and money and obviously affected my motivation. In a while, I gave up and was back to where I started.

I tried dieting for a short time of period, which seemed too hard to keep up with, and I fell back to old unhealthy habits. I was so desperate to lose weight. I wasn't able to figure out what was I doing wrong? I thought I was moving in the correct direction. I was finding it difficult to understand my body system. I gained twice as much as I lost every time. I was quite frustrating.

Inspiration story solution excellent results

I realized this was going to be one of the most challenging life tasks I had to face. I thought to myself, "why is weight so easy to gain, yet it's hard to lose"? It is definitely, because of the popular saying, "an old habit dies hard". I gained so much weight that according to the BMI, I was officially falling in the category of obese. I should have done something about it, but I did not take any concrete action until something drastic happened.

In 2014, it was summers, I started to begin a sudden intense pain in my abdomen that usually lasted over an hour. The pain was excruciating to the extent that I had to go for medical examination where my fear became apparent. I was diagnosed with a high level of cholesterol reading of 7.9. The cause behind the pain was Gallstones formed due to cholesterol. This condition triggered an intense abdominal pain that usually lasts around 1 to 5 hours. This pain is known as Biliary Colic and is mostly treated with painkillers that I used often to ease the pain, but that wasn't the cure. I decided to find out more about GALLSTONES.

What are Gallstones?

They are not actual stones; they are pieces of solid particles formed of bile, cholesterol, and bilirubin in the gallbladder (a small pear-shaped sack-like organ located under the liver in the upper right part of the abdomen). These stones are formed when the amount of cholesterol in the bile is elevated. You might not even have a clue for their presence until they block a bile duct, thereby causing much pain, which would require immediate medical treatment.

Gallstone varies in sizes and actually becomes a problem when one or more of the stone clogs the opening of the duct outside the gallbladder. This can trigger a sudden intense abdominal pain that usually known as Biliary Colic.

Common Symptoms of Gallstones

Following are few symptoms pointing towards gallstones that are not relieved by over the counter medications:

✓ Intense abdominal pain

(I.S.S.E.)

Inspiration story solution excellent results

- ✓ Fever and sweating
- ✓ Chills
- ✓ Jaundice
- ✓ Nausea and vomiting

Key risks factors for Gallstone formation

It is also important to point out the main two key factors that could lead to the formation of cholesterol gallstones. Usually, our focus is mainly on the first factor while the second should also be taken into consideration, especially when you commence your weight loss journey:

- ✓ Being overweight
- ✓ Rapid weight loss on a crash or starvation diet

Health and Physical Challenges

Over time, I started experiencing such intense pain resulting from gallbladder attacks that I could not breathe properly. The pain is commonly located at your back, either between your shoulder blades or in your right shoulder. I was experiencing all the earlier mentioned symptoms. The pain bugged me in the middle of the night. The only remedy was painkillers that provided little or no help since the pain was so intense and unbearable.

The Pain got so worse that I end up in hospital and surgery was the only viable option available to save my life. After surgery, I asked the doctor what caused the problem; the doctor told me all was the diet-related problem, resulting from long-term bad eating habits.

Due to all these health problems, I spent a lot of time going in and out of the hospital. I can recall coming out of the operating room one new year's eve, the moment I opened my eyes, all I heard was doctors and nurse saying to each other the new year's greetings, while lying on the hospital bed, it suddenly dawned on me that the blame for my condition was all on me. I decided to do something about my problem as soon as I recover. At all cost, I must do something proactive to reduce and monitor my weight, which will over time, improve my health.

I have had enough of being overweight, I decide, if I don't

(I.S.S.E.)

Inspiration story solution excellent results

change my lifestyle and eating habits, I will probably end in the hospital again with an even worsened situation, I have suffered enough in the past due to my negligence in handling my health challenges.

A second encounter I had, which I call the 'Icing on the cake' that made me realize that the negligence of my health does not only affect me but also my family/loved ones. It happened on a fateful day when my little princess came up to me and said "dad I love you so much, you went through a lot in the past due to your health, it had a serious effect on us, so I do not want to lose you. Is it ok if you can shed or lose some weight?" I was shocked. She concluded by saying in a joking manner; "dad, you look like my granddad, please make sure you look like my dad soon, everyone thinks you are my granddad". This conversation was life-changing for me; it inspired me, even more, to do something urgently about my weight and health.

At that moment, I felt disappointed in myself. I have let the family and myself down. My kids were concerned about my health. I looked at her and said, "Don't worry princess, this time I will make sure that I look like your dad, not your granddad". She replied; "that would be a dream come true for me".

The game was on, and I was ever so determined. From that day onward, I had no choice but to engage myself in the pursuit of my weight loss agenda. I did some research on how to lose weight in a healthy way, no more supplement or shortcuts. I realized the process of losing weight takes time and requires patience to succeed, and there's no need to rush.

How Can I Lose Weight?

Questions began to spring up in my mind, what do I do next? Where do I go? Whom do I believe? If I do not take the necessary action, now history will repeat itself. I was in a desperate situation and ready to do whatever it takes.

I failed miserably in the past, I cannot afford to fail this time around, the word failure had to be sponged from my

(I.S.S.E.)

Inspiration story solution excellent results

dictionary, no more excuses, no lazier approach towards my intended project, I knew it was going be very challenging, so I had to put my head down and face my fears

Fear as an abbreviation has two meanings (false, evidence appealing real) or (fear, everything, and run), so I decided to face my biggest fear and accept all the challenges that come along with it. I knew it would not be easy, but I was willing to sacrifice my comfort to achieve my goals. I had to improve myself a little every single day, and eventually, there will be some significant changes for sure.

Why am I doing this?

I am doing this for my family and most importantly for myself, so I can live a healthy, long and happy life with my family. From July 15th 2017, I started my weight loss journey, this fruitful journey that has changed my life for good, and I will never forget that day. This time there is no such thing as giving up or going back, no excuses, junk food and no more laziness. Action as is popularly said "speaks louder than words". On that faithful day, I embarked on my mission with a positive mindset. After a year of perseverance, hard work while striving to make the mark, I began to notice that, I have become very energetic and light. It came to my realization that I was shedding fat and shedding weight like never before; the results were amazing and very fulfilling. Close friends and family members started noticing the wonderful change, after a year of determination, hard work and rigorous routine from 15 July 2017 to 15 July 2018, I shed 100 lb. (45Kg) of my weight.

After a year of committed hard work, I was finally happy because I could see the difference and attest to the visible results of my labour, I had to empty out my wardrobe simply because my clothes no longer fit me. On a particular occasion, I attended the parents and teacher association at my kid's school, and the teachers could hardly recognize me. They actually thought I was someone else, all of sudden I was at the centre of attention, and everyone wanted to know how I manage to lose so much in such a short space of time. My own neighbours also could not recognize me.

At another occasion, while I was on a trip, I was stopped by immigration passport control, I have pulled aside for questioning to confirm my identity. It took them a while to confirm, but at the end of the exercise, they realized that I was the same person on the passport who has undergone a little transformation. I had to explain that I lost so much weight as a health precaution. The officer recommended that I update my passport photo. This time around, I did not disappoint my family or myself. I felt like the wealthiest man in the world, as they say; your health is your wealth.

Based on my success so far, I would be sharing my understanding and knowledge garnered in my quest to lose weight and how I succeeded in such a short time. One of the reasons I decided to write this book is for other people to understand how I did it and what informed my decision to take action and if possible, apply the same formula as I did to get that astounding results.

What helped me most was a determination for taking the necessary and prompt actions. Secondly, focusing on how to achieve my vision every day also helped. I had to plan and actively pursue my daily, weekly, monthly and annual goals. Even when I was knocked down in life, the only choice that I had was to get up and move forward, and I realised I do not have time to waste. I decided to wake up every day at the same time, exactly 5:30, start with meditation for 10 minutes; this is how I used to meditate:

- ✓ Take a 5-seconds long deep breath, and then hold it for 5 seconds, then breathe out slowly for 5 seconds,
- ✓ Do the actions for a set of 11 rounds, then

clear your head while meditating. It helped me improve my focus.

Thirdly, I had to focus on the present and not the past, I knew exactly what my number one goal was, so I always kept that in mind and fit it into my daily lifestyle schedules. It became a habit, 10 minutes' meditation, after which I will go for an hour walk. I started from the basic, and gradually I worked my way up, first thing first, I do drink a glass of mineral water before I start walking, when I am done, I will then have my breakfast, which is a finger of banana, two boiled eggs and glass of water. For lunch, it would be a hand full of couscous vegetables such as chickpeas, broccoli, carrots, sweet corn, spinach, chicken breast with skin off, fish and plain water, and for dinner, I would have one apple or orange and plain water. I did this consistently for a year!

For a year? You might ask, yes for a year. Sometimes in life, you need to push yourself beyond the boundaries and out of your comfort zone in order to achieve your goals, and this would not be easy. I used to go to the gym 3 times during the week with my coach William Canty who helped me a lot. Coaches help you reach your goals faster. In life, whether you are doing business or losing weight, having a coach to motivate and direct makes a lot of difference. I believe that with their help, you can reach your goals faster. I tried to lose weight in the past and failed so many times, failure is not a bad thing though, you just learn and grow from it, I never gave up although I failed many times in the past. I learned a lot from my failures, and finally, I lost 100 lbs. within a year! For me, that was the biggest achievement! All the struggles I went through, and the hard work paid off, pain is just temporary; it does not last forever. Now I am happy with my life.

My Simply Stay Away (SSA) List

At the onset of and through your weight loss journey, you would need to stay away from the following:

(I.S.S.E.)

Inspiration story solution excellent results

- ❖ Deep Frying: such as chips. Chicken burger, lamb burger, beef burger, lamb donner, chicken donner, crisps etc.
- ❖ Sweets: cupcake, biscuit, ice cream, chocolate bars, Muffin, cake etc.
- ❖ Drinks: energy drinks, Lucozade, Red bull, Coca-Cola, 7up. Fanta, Mirinda, Pepsi coke, diet coke, juice, alcohol etc.
- ❖ Flour: white bread, pasta, pizza, breadstick, cereals, cookies, crackers etc.

I do understand how difficult it is to stay away from these types of foods. Apply these rules and follow it rigorously, and you will see that big change that you have dedicated your resources to attain. So you have two options, you can either take unflinching action or forget about losing weight. If you really want to have real changes in your life, do not wait for it. I know one thing for sure, you can get your physique into what you desire, but self-discipline and consistency are indispensable tools. More solutions will be discussed in the next chapter.

CHAPTER THREE:
Solution

In solving the challenge of excessive weight, it would be very important to understand the things we do or do not do that result in the weight gain and what we must begin to do to effect the necessary changes. In this chapter, I talked about Leptin, which is produced by fat cells and plays a major role in regulating when we stop eating and increasing and decreasing our metabolic rates. I also talked about leptin resistance which results from lack of proper management of the leptin levels and how knowing how to reset and control your leptin level would help control excessive weight gain.

Secondly, I also touched on the issue of our nutrition, which involves not only what we eat but also how we prepare what we eat. That is the methods used such as air frying/grilling instead of deep-frying with oil, steaming rather than boiling our food. In addition, the importance of the cookware we use for preparing our food and how they affect our overall health and wellbeing.

Now let us dive in.

What is Leptin, and how does it work?

Leptin is the master hormone that regulates body weight and is also referred to as the "Starvation or satiety hormone". It is a protein that is produced in fat cells in our body in proportion to body-fat levels: the much fat you have, the more leptin is produced. It enters the bloodstream via your circulatory system, leptin binds to protein in the blood, and when leptin reaches capillaries in the brain, it travels across the blood-brain barrier. Leptin lets your hypothalamus know when it is time for you to stop eating, then it increases your metabolic rate in order to achieve energy balance (known as homeostasis). Conversely, leptin also tells us when to eat – when you

(I.S.S.E.)
Inspiration story solution excellent results

have less body fat, fewer leptin signals the brain, and you get the message "I am hungry!"

Treating a hormone badly, there are always consequences. By consuming fewer calories, exercise, and burning more fat, you create the gateway for weight loss, but that strategy only goes that far. Over time, calories deprivation contributes to lower leptin levels and slows down your metabolism, making it virtually impossible to lose all the weight you want. Leptin can also bite back if you ignore it, over-eating beyond normal energy maintenance levels harms your body's ability to distinguish whether your fat levels are too high or not, the worst part is your leptin receptors in the brain become numb to the "stop eating" warning resulting in Leptin Resistance.

What causes leptin resistance?

The cause of leptin resistance stems mainly from inflammation and inflammatory signaling in the hypothalamus. It is likely an important cause of leptin resistance in both animals and humans. Fatty acids in the bloodstream may increase fat metabolites in the brain and interfere with leptin signaling. Potential causes of leptin resistance include inflammation, elevated free fatty acids and high leptin levels. All three are factors of obesity increase.

Ripple effect of leptin resistance

As excessive eating continues due to leptin resistance, leptin resistance also becomes predictive of insulin resistance, which may mean that leptin plays a role in controlling insulin sensitivity. Insulin sensitivity can lead to type 2 diabetes and obesity. Leptin and thyroid are frenemies (friends and enemies). The thyroid and leptin have a precarious but meaningful relationship; your thyroid secretes hormones that act throughout the body, influencing metabolism, growth and development. The amount of leptin available to your brain has a major influence on how many thyroid hormones are released into the body.

Inspiration story solution excellent results

Leptin holds the purse strings on your energy spend, based on our available food supply. When your body cannot use leptin efficiently, it goes into a fake starvation mode known as leptin resistance. Leptin Resistance throws a monkey wrench into your thyroid function. Leptin tells the TRH (thyroid releasing hormone) in your hypothalamus to set the thyroid hormones on low energy; otherwise the body may perish from starvation. In turn, the hypothalamus affects how much TSH (thyroid stimulating hormone) your pituitary gland will produce.

Subsequently, your brain unwittingly depresses your metabolism so that you can survive a faulty famine, making weight loss nearly impossible and even promoting weight gain, and, you will be tired all the time because when your thyroid is low, you make less energy in your cells. You feel like a flashlight with only half a battery left.

Researchers also believe that small elevations in TSH may indicate a leptin and insulin problem connected to weight gain, rather than a thyroid problem, leptin-influenced weight gain can inflame the thyroid and invite the production of thyroid antibodies, which aggravate the gland. It is possible that leptin resistance leads to Hashimoto disease.

Now, the GOOD NEWS: you can reset your leptin sensitivity!

Fasting

Fasting is one of the major ways to reset Leptin levels. It is designed to keep inflammation and triglycerides low by limiting fructose, eliminating toxins, and reducing food rewards and cravings, all of which reset leptin levels and allow for effortless weight loss. Leptin levels also drop during short term fasting and return to normal after eating, making it one of the reasons why fasting is a painless but powerful way to retain leptin sensitivity.

Fasting promotes longevity in animals and humans:

Fasting can improve cholesterol levels by reducing LDL (bad cholesterol) and blood triglycerides. It gently stresses your cells, making them more resilient. This includes neurons (brain cells), it can also promote autophagy in your neurons – that's when they get rid of damaged cells, toxins, and waste. Autophagy is partially responsible for the boost in mental clarity you may experience during fasting. If you have tried fasting, you know that it works, and that, it is inconvenient because you run out of energy right in the middle of your day, and you don't enter ketosis (fat-burning mode) fast enough.

Fasting sparingly until your leptin sensitivity has returned, consume healthy fats and protein in the morning to create building blocks for your hormones and eliminating fructose and sugar of any kind from your diet as well as stopping the intake of refined or processed foods can make a significant difference in your weight loss journey.

Overall purpose and benefits of fasting

The core purpose of this fasting is to reset your system mentally and physically. It resets your whole body and brain system. As it gets rid of the toxins from your body, it also boosts your brain cells. For those who are suffering from depression, anxiety, worries, amnesia, low self-esteem etc., it helps you clear your mind. You will be more focused; you begin to build up your self-confidence. Let us say you have a room full of junk and you keep adding more each day, over a long span of time, what do you think will happen? It will be full of junk. So what is the solution?

You have to clean the room-clearing all of the unwanted elements before reinstating to its previous state. This will take some time. You have to throw out all the trash and clean the room, then put in place air freshener, or lit some candles to change the mood and atmosphere to enable you to relax in that room. Same with our brain, we load our brain with all unwanted elements that are why this fasting is good for the brain, it clears the brain of all the unwanted information, gives you a brain boost, powering

(I.S.S.E.)

Inspiration story solution excellent results you to think positive and sharp.

It helps you physically, it clears your system internally, and your bloodstream as well. It helps a lot with the leptin level. You will feel so light and right, that is why I highly recommend fasting to those who can do it. I am not saying it is easy, after one week, your system will get used to it, and all the junk and toxic that got into your body will be cleared off completely. This fasting procedure played a major role in my weight loss program; it helped me physically and mentally. With the fasting coupled with strict adherence to dieting, I was losing weight so fast. I was amazed at the results.

This fasting has changed my whole life, within 12 months, though I used 6 months, I only fasted for 3 months in row, I was taking a syrup prepared using a mug of hot water, one tablespoon of apple cider vinegar, fresh organic lemon and tablespoon of shredded ginger and a little raw honey to taste. In the last 3 months, I had undergone rigorous exercising, such as skipping, boxing, weight lifting, and biking, walking, running, press-ups as well as sit-ups that is what worked for me. I am not saying it will be easy but if you are willing to take on these challenges why not, the result will most certainly be worth it. If you want to have changes in your life, you have to develop the will power to do so.

The Downside of Plain Fasting;

For all its benefits, plain fasting is not all sunshine and rainbows. Starving yourself for long hours takes extra effort, you get hungry, distractingly hungry, with hunger comes the loss of focus, grumpiness, and decreased productivity, and that's no fun for anyone. This is one of the most powerful modes of fasting that helped me a lot. Personally, you fast today and go off the next day that means you fast throughout the year, 6 months on and 6 months off. The way it works like you fast today, next day no fasting, this can be likened to you fasting on Monday and not fasting on Tuesday, the trend follows for

(I.S.S.E.)

Inspiration story solution excellent results

Wednesday and Thursday.

You can begin your fasting just before the sunrise, and you break your fasting after sunset. While you are fasting, you do not eat or drink anything whatsoever. After sunset when I am breaking my fast, I usually start with

Eating 3 fresh dates, drink plain water and wait for 5 minutes,

I then eat mix vegetables, such as fresh carrot, broccoli, spinach, mushroom, tomatoes, green peas and sweet corn, (steamed)

Followed by one steak size skinless chicken breast or fish and one handful of couscous or white plain rice.

I then wait for 2 hours, just eat one orange/apple, and I am done for the day.

In addition, you would also need to avoid high lectin foods because lectins from food can cause leptin resistance. Limiting your carb intake during the day and eating to eliminate food cravings will give your liver and hormones a rest. Your liver needs to use gluconeogenesis again when you are awake and asleep. It is important to note that snacking destroys the timing and circadian clocks which works in unison with leptin. Therefore, it is vital to allow 4-5 hours between foods to ensure the effectiveness of the circadian clocks.

You must also make sure you are getting enough Omega 3 in your diet from grass-fed meat, fish or chicken. I also found out that eating 5 pieces of almonds nuts or any other types of nuts you prefer can help to reduce cravings/hunger. Although some people are nut allergic and would need to avoid eating nut but could find other suitable and healthy alternatives. Furthermore, you would need to contact your doctor about anything in this book; you are not sure you should practice.

Another vital aspect to resetting your leptin levels is SLEEP. You must make sure you get enough sleep; 7 to 8 hours daily. For severe cases, get to bed by 10 pm each night and optimize your sleep. Avoid counting calories; let the food do the healing. You might ask, "How will I know it is working"? Now that the formula is laid out, it is vital to note that, most people experience weight loss quickly, but some people take a few weeks to get it going. Therefore, you must practice patience in this weight loss journey, but your mood should improve, and your sleep quality will increase, especially if you monitor it. You should also get a lot more energy enough for you to want to work out, and you still feel good when you are done.

Finally, taking control of your leptin is one of the most useful and practical approaches to owning your metabolic system.

The following are useful summary facts to note about Leptin:

It is the main hormone responsible for losing and gaining weight.

It is responsible for sending signals to the brain when to eat or not to eat.

Leptin is carried by the bloodstream into the brain.

Leptin resistance may be the main biological abnormality in obesity.

Obese people have a high level of leptin or have an active leptin resistance condition.

Leptin is now believed to be the leading driver of fat gain in human,

Leptin main role is long-term regulation of an energy balance.

If you have body fat, especially in the belly area, then you are almost certain that you are leptin resistance, which results in:

Continuous excessive eating and more leptin resistance;

Resulting in; even more excess weight gain and a dangerous issue.

You need to make sure your leptin is reset and

Learn how to control your leptin.

Fasting is one of the best ways to reset your leptin.

Sleeping well works wonders.

(I.S.S.E.)

Inspiration story solution excellent results

Taking in more protein and less carbohydrates is vital

Consuming fewer calories and exercising to burn more fat.

Avoid any processed and deep-fried foods.

We need to learn how to control our leptin.

We need to understand that obese people have a lot of body fat in their fat cells because fat cells produce leptin in proportion to their size, obese people like me also have a very high level of leptin. Given the way leptin is supposed to work, these people should not be eating; their brain should know that they have plenty of energy stored; however, the problem is that the leptin signal system has become faulty resulting in leptin resistance. This is now believed to be the main biological abnormality in human obesity. When the brain doesn't receive the leptin signals, it erroneously thinks that the body is starving, even though it has more than enough energy stored, this makes the brain change our physiology and behavior in order to regain the fat that the brain thinks we're missing.

The brain begins to act in the following ways:

Eating more: the brain thinks that we must eat so that we do not starve to death.

Reduced energy expenditure: the brain thinks we need to conserve energy, so it makes us feel lazier and makes us burn fewer calories at rest.

In this way, eating more and exercising less is not the cause of weight gain; it is the effect of leptin resistance, a hormonal defect. For the great majority of people, trying to exert cognitive inhibition (will power) over the leptin-driven starvation signal is next to impossible. The bottom line is people who are obese have a high level of leptin, but the leptin signal is faulty resulting in leptin resistance, which can cause hunger and reduce energy expenditure.

This is the reason why losing weight, deuces leptin, so the brain tries to gain the weight back. Most "diets" do not provide good long-term results. This is a well-known problem in weight loss studies. Diets are so ineffective that

Inspiration story solution excellent results
whenever someone goes from obese to thin, it is seen as newsworthy material. The truth is, when it comes to losing weight, long-term success is the exception, not the rule. There are many possible reasons for this, but the research shows that leptin may have a lot to do with it. Losing weight reduces fat mass, which leads to a significant reduction in leptin levels. However, the brain does not necessarily reverse its leptin resistance.

In this weight loss journey, it is therefore vital to correct and continually control this abnormality by the resetting of our leptin levels by fasting and dieting as earlier discussed. We must also work hard at avoiding most of the lifestyle diseases prevalent today, such as:

Obesity
Cancer
Diabetes
Cardiovascular diseases
Stroke
Cholesterol
Digestive problems

Now you would also agree that all of these aforementioned diseases are on the increase in today's society and they have one thing in common, and they are diet-related. The World Health Organization (WHO) says the best cure for most of these diseases is prevention and one of the reasons we contract these diseases are lack of proper nutritional diet. That is why they say, we, in the so-called modern world are the most overfed but highly malnourished generation that has ever lived.

Exercising

Lastly, the role of exercising cannot be completely ruled out in this journey of weight loss. As you are doing everything necessary to ensure effective weight loss, you must also include exercising to the process. Exercise is a planned, structured physical activity that helps to increase the daily body metabolism, burn a little bit more calories and also help to maintain and increase lean body mass, which also helps increase the number of calories you burn each day.

I will not be dwelling a lot on what exercise you need to do and how frequently you would need to exercise as it differs for individuals. My advice would be for you to engage a personal trainer who can work with you to develop a routine that works for your body type/structure and your daily schedule.

Exercising was a vital part of my weight loss journey, and I did engage the input of a personal trainer to ensure I maximized the physical activities I was involved with, and it turned out well for me. During my exercise sessions, I did practice the following, which I believe might be useful for you but you would still need to explore more techniques that are specific to your needs and can deliver a significant result for you:

Tips:

Make sure you do some stretches before and after your exercise sessions

Go on the treadmill, start walking for 2 minutes on a speed of 5.2km

Increase the speed to 10.2km for 3 minutes, then bring the speed back to 5.2km for one minute of walking and then stop the treadmill

Start with lightweight full-body workouts for 45 minutes. Once you complete the full-body workout, jump back on the treadmill, start walking on a speed of 5.2km for 1 minute.

Increase the speed to 10.2km for 3 minutes, then lower the speed to 5.2km for 1 minute and then stop the treadmill

Finally, do some stretches and you are done for the day

Make sure you do these exercises for 5 days and rest for 2 days before you start again.

It is important to note that simplicity and consistency

Inspiration story solution excellent results always goes a long way in making a huge difference in your weight loss journey.

In the next segment, I take a quick look at nutrition, touching on what we eat and how the way we prepare our food can affect the amount of nutrition we get from them.

Our food nutrition

Now there are three main reasons why we eat food;

We eat to satisfy our hunger.

We eat to appease our curious taste buds.

We eat to harness the nutritional component of the food for our body metabolisms needed to keep us fit and healthy.

The six enemies to proper nutrition

Nutritional experts confirm that the average home can lose many of the nutritional components in their food because of how they prepare the food and the types of cookware used for its preparation.

These are the main enemies of nutrition.

Peeling: anything that's grown under the ground, has the vitamins are just under the skin. Above ground, in the centre, many of the nutrients in vegetables can be found just under the skin, and when we peel them, we lose a lot of the goodness.

Water: many vitamins and minerals are water-soluble, and water leaches them out of the food. That is why the water changes colour when you cook vegetables, e.g. peas (green) and salt, which is mineral, dissolves.

Oxidation: air and light can strip the goodness from our food. When you bite an apple and put it on the side what happens? It changes colour, so if we do not cook in an airtight container, we can lose even more nutrition. Nutritionists say if you can smell your food when it is cooking. You can smell vitamins and minerals, leaving your food.

High heat: we put our food in a saucepan; bring it up to boil 1000c. If I wanted to sterilize a baby's feeding bottle, I could boil it in high heat over 100 degrees and would have killed the bacteria. In the same way, anything above 86 degrees could kill the nutrients. Cooking food at 86 degrees is the optimum temperature to kill the bad bacteria but also to maximize the nutrition in your food. So you actually kill the nutrients in your food when we boil our vegetables.

Steaming: steaming is a better procedure than boiling, which occurs at 1000c plus, and it is a wet heat. Although, if you steam excessively, you also lose nutrients in your food. Therefore, it is important to note that when steaming, if you lose the colour, you lose the vitamins, and if you lose the flavour, you lose the minerals.

Fats and oils: These make our food 7-8 times harder to digest, and they give us those extra inches we spent so much time trying to lose. For example, if we deep-fry a chicken or potato in oil/fats and then you empty out the oil in the sink, it definitely gets the sink blocked. That is exactly what will happen to our artery if we keep eating deep-fried and unhealthy food? We eat with our eyes, and we digest with our stomachs, our eyes go like yummy, but our stomach goes what is in it for me? Oh, I already have enough, so I will store it but not in the safest of places but in our arteries.

The body does not just crave for food: it craves for the nutritional minerals we get from the foods. So if we unconsciously end up reducing the vitamins and minerals components in our food, we also end up eating more than necessary or excessively just to compensate for the lack of vitamins and minerals in the food. Have you ever had a meal, stuffed yourself and an hour or two later you are hungry? Now if you stop and think about it, at the back of your mind, you are trying to think why I feel hungry so soon considering you already had a big lunch or big dinner. The truth is, the body is actually searching for all those nutritional elements and discovers we have not had enough to sustain it. Therefore, it sends a signal to the brain saying we need more vitamins and minerals and we

Inspiration story solution excellent results interpret that, as I am hungry. It depends where it catches you, if it catches you at the wrong time, you do not usually land on an apple or banana; rather, it is a packet of crisps or Mars bar. It is always whatever you can get your hands on, can you now understand why they say, "We are the most overfed undernourished generation that has ever lived".

Food preparation Process Improvement

We can actually make significant improvements to our health by improving the process of preparing our food. You must protect your health by eliminating oil and fat, that causes plaque that blocks the artery walls. Why reduced fat in your diet? According to "Choices for a healthy heart" by Joseph C. Piscatell fore worded by Dr Denton A. Cooley, a study found that 1 out of 3 children had a significant risk factor of having a heart attack by the age of 14. In addition, artery blockage greater than 50% was found in children as young as 7 years. Fats and oils are the number one causes of cardiovascular diseases around the world.

Please permit me to be melancholic for a minute, but the chances of dying in a car accident are 1 in 5000. What do you think the chances of contracting a heart-related disease or stroke are? It is actually one in four; it is the biggest killer in the UK. Fat does not just gather around your waist. It also gathers in the bloodstream causing plaque to build up which can block our arteries. By then, the only option you would have is surgery.

How can we avoid using excessive fats and oils during food preparation? Most of the time, our cooking utensils forces us to use oils/fats let me give you some examples, we all use pots and saucepans in our Kitchen.

Lower-grade stainless steel cookware usually has poor heat distribution, are difficult to clean when food burns and stick to hot spots; hence the greater needs for water, oil or fat for cooking.

Copper is most cookware destroy some vitamins

Inspiration story solution excellent results

including vitamin c and folic acid when they come in contact with such foods. Poor heat distribution, breakable surface, can cause food to stick and burn. This also affects the nutritional components of our food

Cast iron characteristics are rough surface; under a microscope, it looks just like a sponge-rancid and food can collect in its pores. Cast iron cookware was designed to be used on outdoor burners, after cooking they would put into the flames to burn it off. Now we just put it back in the cupboard full of old food and oil that will rust when washed unless oiled.

Aluminium cookware used to be very popular but not so much these days. Since the 60s disdain, a circumstantial link between Alzheimer's disease and aluminium and I suppose many people have thought; it is better safe than sorry.

Nonstick Teflon and Tefal are the two main non-stick brands, and they are plastic. The real name is polytetrafluoroethylene. When heated to a temperature just a bit higher than the temperature required for crisping beef, it gives off up to 6 toxic chemicals. The fumes are given off cause something known as polymer fume fever which causes flu-like symptoms in human which lasts a couple of days. It can also be fatal to small Birds like budgerigars and parrots.

Do a Google search for Teflon health hazards" and have a look at what comes up it is quite amazing. If you look at the small print on a new Tefal pan, it tells us to throw the pan away if it is cracked, chipped or flaked, which suggest that it is not quite safe to use.

Possible solutions to these problems

Research has revealed using Titanium cookware is the healthiest ways to cook your food. 316 ti titanium surgical stainless steel is highest grade available, Swiss and the USA, used in operations, for screws and pins and by dentists. It does not react to the body and will not react with enzymes and acid in food. It is quite easy to clean, a

(I.S.S.E.)
Inspiration story solution excellent results

bit on the expensive side, but it would be eventually worth your investment. I used them myself, and I bought them from a company called salad master.

It took me years of research. My advice is that you do your own research as well and decide if it is something you want to invest in. The reason why I recommend this is because I use to suffer from dislocation shoulder, the doctors decide to do an operation, and they put two screws in my shoulder to prevent it from dislocation. I have titanium screws inside me for quite a while now. It does not react to the human body, so if it does not react to the human body, then it will not react with acid and enzymes in your food.

Since I started using this 316 ti titanium cookware, my cholesterol level went down faster, because the cookware does not need fat or oil to cook with, so whatever you put in the pan is what you get out. Thanks to salad master, it has played an important role in my weight loss project. In the last chapter is where I will be talking about how to get excellent results.

CHAPTER FOUR: Excellent result

To get an outstanding result in losing weight, consistency is the key. Make sure you have a routine in place and repeat daily, of course, you are not going to see results after just week of dieting and exercising but don't give up, one thing I can assure you if you keep doing it daily and with consistency, you will definitely reach your goal.

As long as you set a goal and follow it religiously even when you do not feel like it on some days, you would have to push yourself to achieve that the body and health you always desired. Write down your daily, weekly, monthly and annual goals. Have a vision and clarity and do whatever it takes to achieve them, and make sure you do it consistently. If you must attain an excellent result, you must never give up your dreams and goals. As long as you follow your plan on a consistent basis and keep pushing towards your goals, you will certainly get excellent results. I know this for sure, through my personal experience that ANYTHING IS POSSIBLE, so GO FOR IT!

Here are 11 more tips to lose weight even faster on a consistent base:

1. Eat a high-protein based breakfast.
2. Avoid sugary drinks and fruit juice. These are the most fattening things you can put into your

(I.S.S.E.)

Inspiration story solution excellent results body, and avoiding them can help you lose weight.

3. Drink plain mineral water before a meal at least an hour before.
4. Choose weight loss-friendly foods; certain foods are very useful for losing fat.
5. Eat soluble fiber. Studies show that soluble fiber may reduce fat, especially in the belly area. Fiber supplements like galactomannan can also help.
6. Drink coffee or tea. If you are a coffee or tea drinker, then drink as much as you want as the caffeine in them can boost your metabolism by 3 –11%.
7. Eat mostly whole, unprocessed foods base, most of your diet must be from whole foods. They are healthier, more filling and much less likely to cause overeating.
8. Eat your food slowly. Fast eaters gain more weight over time. Eating slowly makes you feel full faster and boosts weight-reducing hormones.
9. Weigh yourself every day. Studies show that people who weigh themselves every day are much more likely to lose weight and keep it off for a long time.
10. Get good sleep, every night. Poor sleep is one of the strongest risk factors for weight gain, so taking care of your sleep is extremely important.

(I.S.S.E.)

Inspiration story solution excellent results

11. Vegetables and fruits have several properties that make them effective for weight loss; they contain few calories but a lot of fiber. Their high water content gives them low energy density, making them very filling.

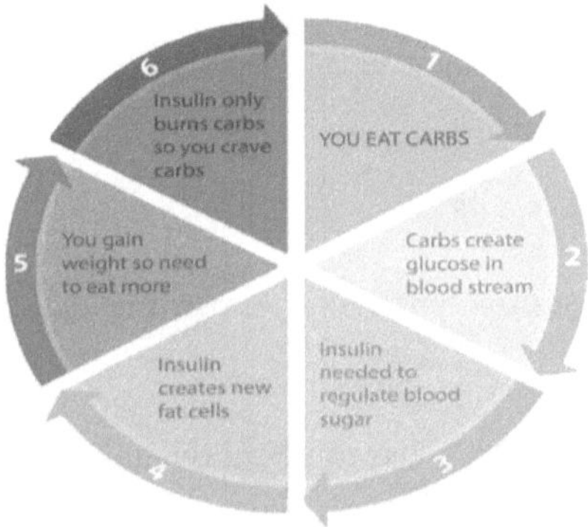

These are all the tools that I developed and deployed very effectively. This is how I got outstanding results. For me, losing 100 lbs. after a year of struggles was my biggest achievement so far in my history of trying to lose weight. I finally made it. All the struggles I went through have paid off, all the cravings, all the hunger, and now I can finally say it is worth it. I do hope you too can say the same at the end of your journey.

(I.S.S.E.)
Inspiration story solution excellent results

The book talks about my story in the four thematic areas that interestingly spells my name: I.S.S.E -

Inspiration

Story

Solution

Excellent results

Let us just do a quick recap of the peculiar rules to adhere to;

1. You need to be motivated and do whatever it takes.
2. You need to have enough information so that you know exactly what to do to lose weight.
3. Make sure you have a solution to all your problems.
4. Make sure you never give up.

Hope you enjoyed the read. I wish you the best of luck in your weight loss journey.

www.ingramcontent.com/pod-product-compliance
Lightning Source LLC
Chambersburg PA
CBHW032132050726

47590CB00008B/3050